Math Counts

Counting

Children's Press®

An Imprint of Scholastic Inc.

About This Series

In keeping with the major goals of the National Council of Teachers of Mathematics, children will become mathematical problem solvers, learn to communicate mathematically, and learn to reason mathematically by using the series Math Counts.

Pattern, Shape, and *Size* may be investigated first—in any sequence.

Sorting, Counting, and *Numbers* may be used next, followed by *Time, Length, Weight,* and *Capacity.*

—Ramona G. Choos, Professor of Mathematics,
Senior Adviser to the Dean of Continuing Education, Chicago State University;
Sponsor for Chicago Elementary Teachers' Mathematics Club

Author's Note

Mathematics is a part of a child's world. It is not only interpreting numbers or mastering tricks of addition or multiplication. Mathematics is about ideas. These ideas have been developed to explain particular qualities such as size, weight, and height, as well as relationships and comparisons. Yet all too often the important part that an understanding of mathematics will play in a child's development is forgotten or ignored.

Most adults can solve simple mathematical tasks without the need for counters, beads, or fingers. Young children find such abstractions almost impossible to master. They need to see, talk, touch, and experiment.

The photographs and text in these books have been chosen to encourage talk about topics that are essentially mathematical. By talking, the young reader can explore some of the central concepts that support mathematics. It is on an understanding of these concepts that a student's future mastery of mathematics will be built.

—Henry Pluckrose

Math Counts

By Henry Pluckrose

Mathematics Consultant: Ramona G. Choos, Professor of Mathematics

Children's Press®

An Imprint of Scholastic Inc.

SCHOLASTIC

What number do you get when you count all your fingers and thumbs?

Have you ever counted steps as you go up and down?

Perhaps you learned to count while getting dressed.
How many buttons are still undone?

Perhaps you learned to count by helping to set the table.
How many people are going to eat here?

Counting helps us find out "how many?"
How many chairs are here?

Now count again. How many chairs are here now?
What other things can you count?

Two shoes make a pair. How many pairs can you see here? How many shoes can you see?

What other things come in pairs? How many pairs of socks are here? How many pairs of gloves? How many pairs of boots?

Each number has a shape of its own.
How many of these numbers do you know?

1 2 3

4 5 6 7

8 9 10

Can you place these numbers in the right order?

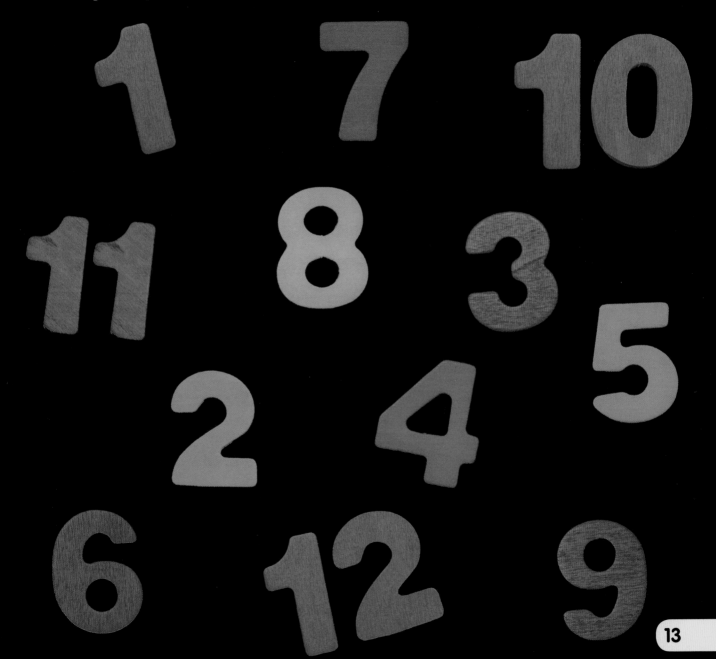

Collect some colored buttons. Make these patterns with them.

Count each pattern. How many buttons are in each pattern?

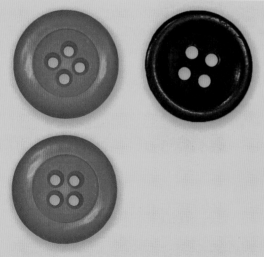

Which pattern gives an *even* number?

Which pattern gives an *odd* number?

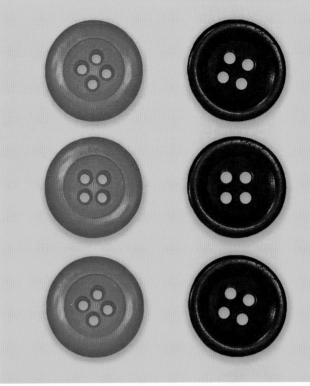

15

How many buttons do you see here?
What sort of pattern can you make
with this number?

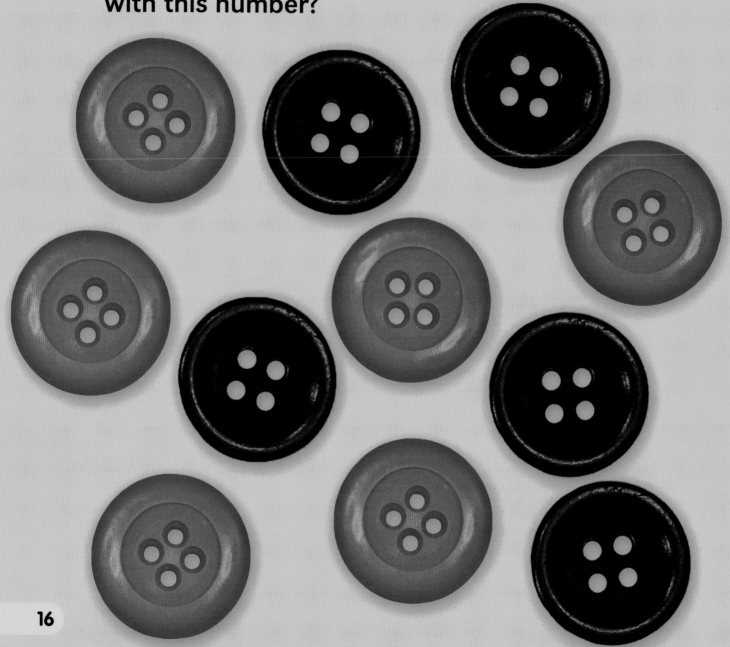

This page is empty.
What number do we use
to show there are
no buttons on this page?

How well can you count?
How many bricks are in this pile?

How many shells
are on this sandy beach?

How many cows are in this picture?
Count their legs.

How many toy people are in this picture?
How many are standing? How many are sitting?

Count these balls.
Are there fewer orange balls than white ones?

Which box contains more eggs?

How many eggs have been taken from each box?

How many have been taken from both boxes?

We count to get an exact answer to the question "How many?" How many strawberries have been bitten?

How many butterflies
are on these flowers?

It is very difficult to count large numbers of things or people. How many people are in this part of the crowd?

It is much easier to count people when they line up.

It is easier to count in ones and twos,

but scientists often have to use very large numbers in their work. How many stars can you count?

Do you know these large numbers?

How did you first learn to count?

Index

Reader's Guide

Visit this Scholastic Web site to download the Reader's Guide for this series:
www.factsfornow.scholastic.com Enter the keywords **Math Counts**

Library of Congress Cataloging-in-Publication Data

Names: Pluckrose, Henry, 1931- author. | Choos, Ramona G., consultant.

Title: Counting/by Henry Pluckrose; mathematics consultant: Ramona G. Choos, Professor of Mathematics.

Other titles: Math counts.

Description: Updated edition. | New York, NY: Children's Press, an imprint of Scholastic Inc., 2019. | Series: Math counts | Includes index.

Identifiers: LCCN 2017061287| ISBN 9780531175071 (library binding) | ISBN 9780531135167 (pbk.)

Subjects: LCSH: Counting—Juvenile literature.

Classification: LCC QA113 .P58 2019 | DDC 513.2/11—dc23

LC record available at https://lccn.loc.gov/2017061287

Copyright © The Watts Publishing Group, 2018

Printed in Heshan, China 62

Scholastic Inc., 557 Broadway, New York, NY 10012.

2 3 4 5 6 7 8 9 10 R 28 27 26 25 24 23 22 21 20 19

Credits: Photos ©: cover: Bianca Alexis Photography; 1: Bianca Alexis Photography; 3: Bianca Alexis Photography; 4: all_about_people/Shutterstock; 5: EvgeniiAnd/Shutterstock; 6: Alina R/Shutterstock; 7: Tim Macpherson/Getty Images; 8-9: Chad McDermott/Shutterstock; 9 umbrellas: Natchapon L./Shutterstock; 9 starfish: Plus69/Shutterstock; 9 pink shell: Alexander Raths/Shutterstock; 9 spiral shell: Scorpp/Shutterstock; 9 bucket: Giovanni Cancemi/Shutterstock; 10 shoes: mediaphotos/iStockphoto; 10 background: majana/iStockphoto; 11 red gloves: Africa Studio/Shutterstock; 11 purple gloves: TerraceStudio/Shutterstock; 11 rainbow socks: Ruslan Kudrin/Shutterstock; 11 green socks: Africa Studio/Shutterstock; 11 blue socks: Evikka/Shutterstock; 11 boot: Lena Nester/Shutterstock; 12: Almaje/iStockphoto; 13: Almaje/iStockphoto; 14-16 blue buttons: Preto Perola/Shutterstock; 14-16 red buttons: Picsfive/Shutterstock; 18: Mike Flippo/Shutterstock; 19: kyoshino/iStockphoto; 20: Photosky/Dreamstime; 21: Dave King/Getty Images; 22: Capture Light/Shutterstock; 23: Amphaiwan/Dreamstime; 23 white egg: Freer/Shutterstock; 24: Jonathan Kantor Studio/Getty Images; 25: ehughes/iStockphoto; 26: Michael Blann/Getty Images; 27: Ken Karp Photography; 28: Pao Laroid/Shutterstock; 29: Arctic-Images/Getty Images; 30: Alain Lacroix/Dreamstime; 31: LWA/Dann Tardif/Getty Images.